Ralph
VAUGHAN WILLIAMS

FANTAISA ON CHRISTMAS CAROLS
(1912)

Edited by
Richard W. Sargeant, Jr.

Vocal Score
Klavierauszug

SERENISSIMA MUSIC, INC.

CONTENTS

Duration: ca. 12 minutes

First performance: September 12, 1912
Hereford Cathedral, Three Choirs Festival
Soli, Festival Chorus, Orchestra
Ralph Vaughan Williams, conductor

ISBN: 978-1-60874-049-9
This score is a newly reserached and engraved edition
prepared by the editor published for the first time.

Printed in the USA
First Printing: September, 2015

Fantasia on Christmas Carols

Ralph Vaughan Williams
Edited by Richard W. Sargeant, Jr.

Andante

Solo Baritone

Piano
pp

Bar.

This is the truth sent from a-bove, The truth of God, the God of love: There-

Pno.

Bar.

17

fore don't turn me from your door, But hear-ken all, both rich and poor. The

S.
pp
(humming tone)

A.
pp
(humming tone)

T.
pp
(humming tone)

B.
pp
(humming tone)

Pno.

17

40499

Bar. first thing which I will re-late Is that God did man cre-ate, The next thing which to

Bar. you I'll tell, Wo-man was made with man to dwell.

(humming tone)

Bar. Then, af - ter this, 'twas

A. (closed lips)

T. Ah _____ (closed lips)

B. (closed lips)

Pno. *mf* cantabile *dim.* *pp*

Bar. God's own choice To place them both in Par - a - dise, There to re - main, from

A.

T. unis.

B. div.

37
Bar.
e-vil free, Ex - cept they ate of such a tree.
S.
pp
(closed lips)
(humming tone)
A.
unis.
(humming tone)
T.
(humming tone)
B.
unis.
(humming tone)
Pno.
pp
42
46
And they did eat, which
div.
Ah
div.
pp

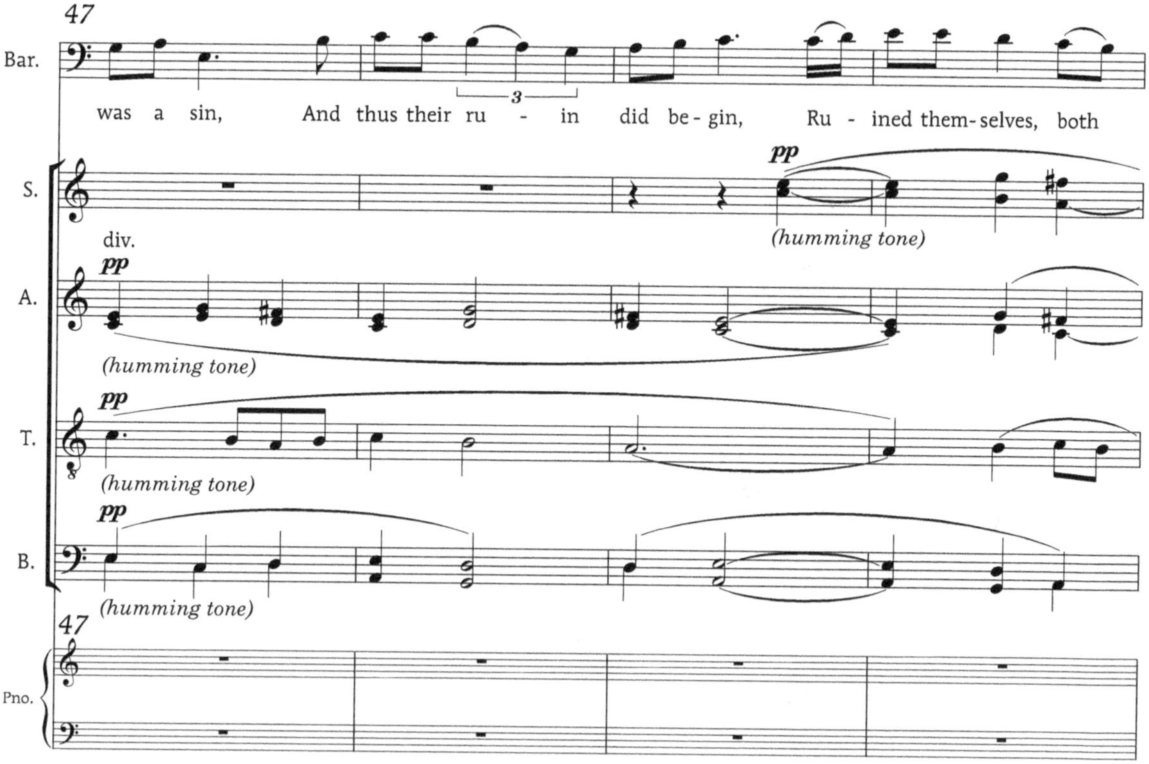
47
Bar.
was a sin, And thus their ru - in did be-gin, Ru - ined them-selves, both
S.
pp
(humming tone)
div.
A.
pp
(humming tone)
T.
pp
(humming tone)
B.
pp
(humming tone)
47
Pno.

51
Bar.
you and me, And all of their pos - ter - i - ty.
S.
mf
Thus
A.
mf
Thus
T.
mf
Thus
unis.
B.
mf
Thus
51
Pno.
p
f

56

Bar.

S.
we were heirs to end-less woes, Till God the Lord did in - ter-pose, And

A.
we were heirs to end-less woes, Till God the Lord did in - ter-pose, And

T.
we were heirs to end-less woes, Till God the Lord did in - ter-pose, And

B.
we were heirs to end-less woes, Till God the Lord did in - ter-pose, And

56

Pno.
p

60

f

Bar.
That he

S.
so a prom - ise soon did run, That he would re - deem us by his Son,

A.
so a prom - ise soon did run, That he would re - deem us by his Son,

T.
so a prom - ise soon did run, That he would re - deem us by his Son,

B.
so a prom - ise soon did run, That he would re - deem us by his Son,

60

Pno.

would re - deem us   by   his Son.

by   his Son.

by   his Son.

by   his Son.

by   his Son.

(closed lips)

(closed lips)

(closed lips)

(closed lips)

75
S.
A.
T.
B.
ppp
ppp
ppp
ppp
Pno.
81
82
Moderato 𝅗𝅥 = 66
mf marc.
Come all you wor - thy gen - tle-men that
mf marc.
Come all you wor - thy gen - tle-men that
p

may be stand-ing by. Christ our bless-ed Sa - viour was born on Christ-mas

may be stand-ing by. Christ our bless-ed Sa - viour was born on Christ-mas

day. The bless-ed Vir-gin Ma - ry un - to the Lord did pray. O we

day. The bless-ed Vir-gin Ma - ry un - to the Lord did pray. O we

The blessed Virgin
The blessed Virgin
wish you the comfort and tidings of joy! The blessed Virgin
wish you the comfort and tidings of joy! The blessed Virgin

Mary unto the Lord did pray. O we wish you the comfort and
Mary unto the Lord did pray. O we wish you the comfort and
Mary unto the Lord did pray. O we wish you the comfort and
Mary unto the Lord did pray. O we wish you the comfort and

106
110
S.
p
tid - ings of joy!
Christ our Bless-ed
A.
p
tid - ings of joy!
Christ our Bless-ed
T.
tid - ings of joy!
B.
tid - ings of joy!
106
110
Pno.
pp
111
S.
Sa - viour now in the man-ger lay He's ly-ing in the man - ger, while the
A.
Sa - viour now in the man-ger lay He's ly-ing in the man - ger, while the
T.
B.
111
Pno.

S. ox - en feed on hay. The bless-ed Vir-gin Ma - ry un - to the Lord did

A. ox - en feed on hay. The bless-ed Vir-gin Ma - ry un - to the Lord did

S. pray. O we wish you the com - fort and tid - ings of joy! The bless-ed Vir-gin

A. pray. O we wish you the com - fort and tid - ings of joy! The bless-ed Vir-gin

T. The bless-ed Vir-gin

B. The bless-ed Vir-gin

127
mf cresc.
S.
Ma - ry un - to the Lord did pray. O we wish
A.
Ma - ry un - to the Lord did pray. O we wish you the com - fort and
T.
Ma - ry un - to the Lord did pray. O we wish
B.
Ma - ry un - to the Lord did pray. O we wish you the com -
Pno.
mf cresc.

132
div.
f
unis.
S.
you the com - - - fort and tid - ings of joy!
A.
tid - ings of joy, tid - ings of joy!
T.
you the com - fort and tid - ings of joy!
B.
fort the com - - - fort and tid - ings of joy!
Pno.
ff

137
S.
tid - ings of joy!
A.
tid - ings of joy!
T.
tid - ings of joy!
B.
tid - ings of joy!
137
Pno.

142
147
S.
com - fort and tid - ings of joy!
f cresc.
A.
com - fort and tid - ings of joy! O we wish,
f cresc.
T.
com - fort and tid - ings of joy! O we wish you the
f cresc.
B.
com - fort and tid - ings of joy! O we wish you the
142
147
Pno.
cresc.

148
S.
A.
T.
B.
Pno.
ff
The blessed Virgin Mary unto the Lord did
we wish you the com - - fort and tid - ings of
com - fort and tid - - - - - ings of joy, O we
com - fort and tid-ings of joy, tid - ings of joy,
153
dim.
pray. O we wish you the com -
joy, O we wish, we wish you the com - fort and tid - -
wish, O we wish you, we wish you the com - - - fort and
O we wish you the com - fort and tid - - - ings, the

158
S.
A.
T.
B.
Pno.
p
pp
- - - fort and tid - - ings of joy!
-ings of joy tid - - ings of joy!
tid - - - - ings of joy tid - ings of joy!
com - fort and tid - ings of joy!
dim.

164
168
S.
A.
T.
B.
Pno.
dim.
pp

On Christ - mas night all Christ - ians sing To hear the news the

an - gels bring.

On Christ - mas night all Christ - ians sing To hear the news the

Ah

Ah

Ah

News of great joy, news of great mirth, an - gels bring. Ah

News of our mer - ci - ful King's birth

News of great

Ah

Ah

Ah

185
Bar.
When
S.
joy, news of great mirth, News of our mer - ci - ful King's
A.
Ah
T.
Ah
B.
Ah
185
Pno.
189
Bar.
sin de-parts be - fore thy grace, Then life and health come in its place.
S.
pp
birth
p
When
A.
pp
(humming tone)
T.
pp
B.
pp
189
Pno.
pp

sin de-parts be-fore thy grace, Then life and health come in its place.

Ah

Ah

An - gels and men with joy may sing, All for to

(humming tone)

201
202 Pocchettino animato
Bar.
see the new - born King.
S.
mf cresc.
All for to see the King
A.
mf cresc.
All for to see the
T.
f
All for to
B.
mf cresc.
All for to see the
Pno.
205
f
All for to see the new - born King the
new - born King All for to see the
see the new - born King An - gels and
new - - - born King

209
S.
ff
new - born King. An - gels and men with joy
A.
ff
King All for to see the new - born King,
T.
ff
men with joy may sing, All for to
B.
ff
An - gels and men with joy may
209
Pno.
ff

213
S.
dim.
may sing to see the new - born
A.
dim.
All for to see the new - born
T.
dim.
see the new - born King.
B.
dim.
sing, All for to see the
213
Pno.
dim.

218
S.
pp
King
A.
pp
King to see the new - born King.
T.
pp
B.
pp
new - born King.
218
Pno.
p dim.
non rall.
226
223
Bar.
f risoluto
God bless the rul - er
S.
A.
T.
B.
223
non rall.
226
Pno.
pp

228
Bar.
of this house and long on may he reign,
S.
pp
Ah
A.
p
From out of dark - ness
T.
pp
Ah
B.
p
From out of dark - ness
228
Pno.
233
Bar.
S.
Ah
A.
we have light, Which makes the an - gels sing this night,
T.
Ah
B.
we have light, Which makes the an - gels sing this night,
233
Pno.

Bar. (236, f): Ma- ny hap- py Christ- mas- es he live to

Bar. (241): see a- gain! From out of dark- ness we have light, Which

S. (241): From out of dark- ness we have light, Which

A. (241): Ah

T. (241): From out of dark- ness we have light, Which

B. (241): Ah

246
244
f
Bar.
God bless our gen - er -
S.
makes the an - gels sing this night,
A.
Ah
T.
makes the an - gels sing this night,
B.
244
246
Pno.
248
Bar.
a - - tion, who live both far and
S.
A.
T.
B.
248
Pno.

252
Bar.
near And we wish them a hap - py, a
S.
Glo - ry to God and peace to men.
A.
Both now and ev - er - more, A -
T.
Glo - ry to God and peace to men.
B.
Both now and ev - er - more, A -
Pno.
256
hap - py New Year.
Both now and ev - er more, A - men.
men. A - men.
Both now and ev - er more, A - men.
men. A - men.

260
263
S.
A.
T.
B.
ff
God bless the rul - er
Pno.
265
of this house And long on may he reign,
ff

Many happy Christmas-es he live to see again!

God bless our gen - er - a - tion, who live both far and near And we wish them a

291
S.
them a hap - py, a hap - py, a
A.
hap - py, a hap - py New Year, a hap - py, a
T.
them a hap - - py, a
B.
hap - py, a hap - py New Year,
Pno.
295
dim.
S.
hap - - py New Year, A hap - py New Year, A
A.
hap - - py New Year, A hap - py New Year.
T.
hap - py, hap - py New Year, A hap - py New Year, A
B.
a hap - py New Year, A hap - py New Year,
Pno.
dim.

300
S.
A.
T.
B.
p
hap - py New Year,
A
p
hap - py New Year,
A
hap - py New Year.
A
300
Pno.
p
304
S.
A.
T.
B.
pp
hap - py New
Year.
p
hap - py New
Year.
304
Pno.

O we wish

321
Bar.
you a hap - py, a hap - py New
S.
ppp
(humming tone)
A.
ppp
(humming tone)
T.
ppp
(humming tone)
B.
ppp
(humming tone)
321
Pno.
326
Bar.
Year.
S.
ppp
Both now and ev - er - more, A - men.
pppp
div.
unis.
A.
ppp
Both now and ev - er - more, A - men.
pppp
div.
T.
ppp
Both now and ev - er - more, A - men.
pppp
div.
B.
ppp
unis.
div.
Both now and ev - er - more, A - men.
pppp
326
Pno.